W9-CYA-539

Shipwrecks of the Explorers

KC Smith

Franklin Watts
A Division of Grolier Publishing
New York • London • Hong Kong • Sydney
Danbury, Connecticut

To Roger, for sharing your love of shipwrecks and seafaring with me from the beginning

Note to readers: Definitions for words in **bold** can be found in the Glossary at the back of this book.

Photographs ©: Archive Photos: 44 (Popperfoto), 4 (USAF Photo), 6, 30; Bridgeman Art Library International Ltd., London/New York: 40 (WCC122196 Pocket chronometer by Vulliamy & Sons, London, and small watch made by Larcum Kendall, London, 18th century/The Worshipful Company of Clockmakers' Collection, UK.); Corbis-Bettmann: 41 (Archivo Iconografico, S. A.), 20, 46; Courtesy of John Harrington: 47; Institute of Nautical Archaeology: 21, 23, 24, 25, 26; Liaison Agency, Inc.: 3 top, 9 (Eric Brissaud), 49 (Hulton Getty); National Geographic Image Collection: 19 (James Sugar); North Wind Picture Archives: 13, 31; Stock Montage, Inc.: 3 bottom, 10, 12, 15, 16, 18, 28, 36, 38; Sygma: 33, 34, 35, 50 (Eranian).

Cover illustration by Greg Harris.

Visit Franklin Watts on the Internet at: http://publishing.grolier.com

Library of Congress Cataloging-in-Publication Data

Smith, KC
    Shipwrecks of the explorers / KC Smith
        p.   cm.— (Watts Library)
    Includes bibliographical references and index.
    Summary: Surveys the archaeological search for the sunken ships of explorers throughout history and discusses the voyages made by the explorers.
    ISBN: 0-531-20378-6 (lib. bdg.)   0-531-16485-3 (pbk.)
    1. Shipwrecks—Juvenile literature. 2. Explorers—Juvenile literature. [1. Shipwrecks. 2. Underwater exploration. 3. Explorers.] I. Title. II. Series.
G525.S573   2000
910'.452—dc21   99-053033

Contents

On May 5, 1961, aboard the Freedom 7, *Alan Shepard became the first U.S. astronaut sent into space.*

Chapter One

Looking for Something New

"Boy, what a ride!" These were Alan Shepard's first words as he emerged from his *Freedom 7* space capsule in the Atlantic Ocean on May 5, 1961. The first U.S. astronaut sent into space, Shepard soared 115 miles (185 kilometers) above Earth at a speed of 5,160 miles (8,302 km) an hour. Flames roared from the 83-foot (25-meter)-long rocket that shot

Shepard aloft at 9:34 A.M. According to one newspaper account, the *Freedom 7* hovered above the launchpad, then lifted skyward "in a heartbeat," propelled by 78,000 pounds (35,412 kilograms) of thrust from the booster engine.

Shepard's one-man mission was a milestone in history. Compared to the voyages of exploration by sailors in ships hundreds of years before, the journey was brief. Shepard splashed down only fifteen minutes later and 302 miles (486 km) away from the launchpad. Five minutes later, he was rescued by a U.S. military helicopter.

Another Epic Event

About 470 years before Shepard's flight, three wooden ships in Palos, Spain, raised their sails to catch the wind and begin an equally important voyage. Christopher Columbus commanded the fleet. Each ship was about 70 feet (21 m) long and carried about thirty crewmen. Two months and two weeks later, the explorers reached an island thousands of miles from home. Unlike the astronaut, they didn't know exactly where they were, and they were greeted by strangers.

Columbus described the departure of his ships—the *Niña*, the

The Niña, *the* Pinta, *and the* Santa María *set sail out of Palos, Spain, in 1492.*

6

Pinta, and the *Santa María*—in his journal. After preparing vessels "well-suited for such an undertaking," he departed "with many provisions and many seamen, on the third day of the month of August . . . at half an hour before sunrise, and took the route for the Canary Islands."

On the Same Course

Although centuries separated their expeditions, Shepard and Columbus had a lot in common. Both men were interested in exploring unknown territory. Both had specific ideas about why they were going, and both were bold enough to make perilous, uncertain journeys. Each set off in vehicles that were revolutionary for their day. Most important, both returned to describe what they had experienced.

Countless other people in history have set out to learn about the world in which they lived. They walked, rode animals, drove wagons, or used watercraft or aircraft. Some were escaping hostilities in their homeland. Some hoped to make a great fortune. Others were sent by governments to acquire new land, establish trade, or spread their beliefs. Still others went simply to go somewhere or do something that no one else had done before.

Many of history's important and famous explorations involved watercraft. Traveling by water permitted people (almost always men) to avoid barriers created on land by nature or by other societies. But this form of transport was risky. Even the best mariners experienced bad weather, hazardous environments, hostile nations, imprecise navigational tools, unhealthy conditions, and worn-out vessels. Many well-planned expeditions returned home with fewer ships and sailors, if they returned at all.

Seeking the Explorers

Today we know about voyages of exploration from documents, maps, and personal accounts. Modern historians conduct research in libraries and **archives** to find and explain these records. Equally valuable information comes from ships that were lost at sea. Underwater **archaeologists** are scientists who find and study shipwrecks and other remains to reconstruct **cultures** and events of the past.

Underwater archaeologists gather evidence to determine where a ship came from, how it was built, why it sailed, what it carried, and why it wrecked. Using precise scientific methods, they map and record the **features** of a site and recover **artifacts**.

When the fieldwork is finished, archaeologists work in libraries and laboratories to explain and analyze what they found. They scour old documents for clues from the past, and they consult other experts. They study the customs of modern maritime cultures to understand seafaring traditions. Archaeologists also subject artifacts to a process called **conservation** to restore objects and ensure that they will be available for future study or display. When the research is completed, they write a detailed report about what they have learned.

Although shipwrecks often look like a pile of junk on the seabed, they are actually time capsules left behind accidentally. Everything on a wreck is a clue to a previous culture. Let's travel the globe to learn about vessels lost by explorers of the past and found by explorers of the present.

Evidence from underwater sites has taught archaeologists much about voyages of exploration.

The Age of Exploration was a time of great maritime activity.

Chapter Two

Exploration Under Sail

The seamen sweated and grunted as they pulled heavy ropes hand over hand to raise the sail at the ship's **bow**. Suddenly, a sharp crack was heard as the wind stretched the huge piece of canvas, ready to guide the ship away from the dock. Sailors hurried to secure the cargo below and the crates on deck filled with animals, destined to be dinner at sea. On the shore, relatives wiped tears from their eyes, and friends said a prayer for a safe and successful voyage.

During the Age of Exploration (A.D. 1450 to 1650), similar scenes were repeated countless times as vessels left European ports to explore, trade, and colonize around the world. The era was important because sailing ships connected many parts of the world for the first time. Humans began to realize how large the world really is.

Legacy of Water Travel

Migration by sea occurred long before the Age of Exploration. About 5,000 years ago, Egyptians made from reeds vessels that were capable of long-distance travel. More than 3,000 years ago, voyagers and traders in wooden boats traveled throughout the Mediterranean Sea. By 600 B.C., the Phoenicians had ventured from the Mediterranean into the Atlantic and had **circumnavigated** the continent of Africa. On the other side of the world, Polynesians began to explore the widely scattered islands of the Pacific Ocean at least 3,000 years ago.

From A.D. 790 to 1100, Viking seafarers explored, traded, and raided in the North Atlantic. They discovered and settled Iceland and Greenland and were the first Europeans to set

Some of the earliest illustrations of watercraft come from Egyptian sources.

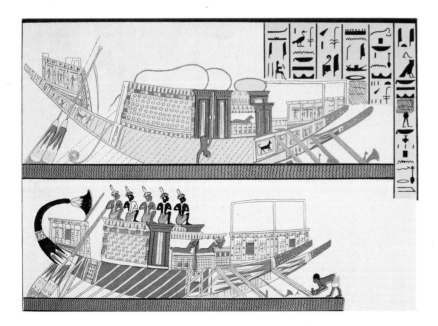

foot in North America. In 1001, explorer Leif Eriksson sailed west from Greenland to Canada. He named the places he reached Helluland, Markland, and Vinland. Vikings tried to settle Vinland, but the colony did not survive. In the early 1960s in Newfoundland, archaeologists found remains of this settlement when they **excavated** at L'Anse aux Meadows in Newfoundland. But if the Vikings were the first people to

Viking mariner Leif Eriksson sailed from Greenland to the coast of North America.

cross the Atlantic successfully, why does Christopher Columbus get credit for this accomplishment?

Perfect Timing

Unlike the Viking voyages, Columbus's expeditions had a lasting effect on world history. They led to permanent European colonies in the Americas and an international exchange of products and ideas. Columbus's timing was perfect. In the fourteenth and fifteenth centuries, Europeans were renewing their interest in science, technology, art, and literature during an era called the Renaissance. People also had grown fond of spices and exotic products from the Orient, which was hard to reach by land. Europe was ready for an age of maritime explorers.

In the early 1400s, the tiny nation of Portugal turned its attention to finding a water route to Asia. Vessels from many nations visited the Portuguese ports, which are strategically located between the Mediterranean Sea and the Atlantic Ocean. **Shipwrights** and sailors gathered the most up-to-date information, which they used to build new types of ships and to improve navigational knowledge. Portuguese mariners explored the west coast of Africa, establishing trading posts as they ventured farther south. In 1488, Bartolomeu Dias finally rounded the southern tip of the African continent, and nine years later, Vasco da Gama sailed all the way on to India.

Portugal controlled the sea lanes around Africa. However, the route to Asia by sailing west was wide open. Christopher

Columbus was the first to attempt this course. When he returned, news of his success spread quickly. Visions of wealth, land, and power attracted other Europeans. But it was soon clear that a continent, not a group of islands, blocked the passage to the Orient. Sailors had to find sea paths around this landmass called America. During the Age of Exploration, many explorers tried.

Christopher Columbus and his crew sighting the Americas in 1492

The Santa María wrecked on the north coast of Hispaniola, an island in the West Indies.

Chapter Three

Miles of Isles

The first recorded shipwreck in the Americas occurred on Christmas Day in 1492. Just after midnight, while Columbus and his crew slept and a cabin boy steered the ship, the *Santa María*—a cargo vessel called a **nao**—slid onto a coral reef so gently that no one awoke. The boy called out an alarm, and sailors rushed on deck to free the stranded craft, but their efforts were useless.

During the next few days, local native peoples helped to remove the ship's cargo and timbers to build a fort on land nearby. A group of men was selected to stay until Columbus could bring a rescue vessel. But when he returned a year later, the fort was in ruins and the men were dead.

Seafaring Hazards

Look at a map of the Caribbean Sea, and you'll understand why it was a challenge to early explorers. A line of large and small islands—from the Bahamas in the north to the Lesser Antilles in the south—creates a natural barrier to the mainland. Most isles are surrounded by dangerous coral reefs and have their own wind and water conditions. Until accurate sea

Early maps of the Caribbean were very inaccurate, causing many vessels to wreck.

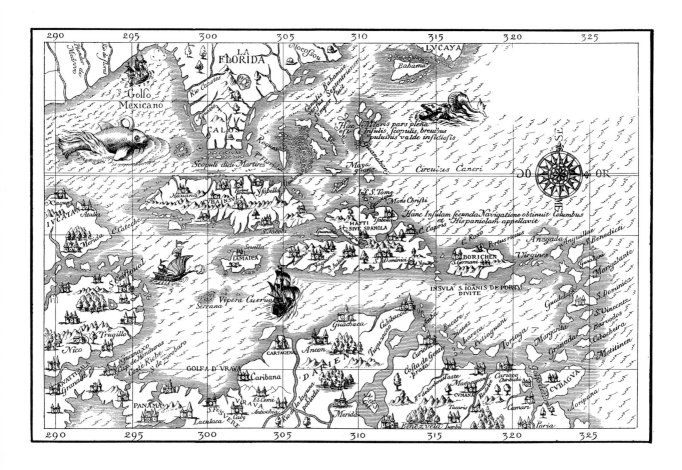

maps were made, mariners were at the mercy of natural hazards. About 120 ships had been lost in the Americas, mostly in the Caribbean, by 1520.

Columbus lost several ships during his four voyages to the Americas. None has ever been found. When the *Santa María* was abandoned, only the **ballast** and lower **hull** were left. Over time, the reef covered these remains, and the shoreline changed so the wreck's location was lost. Searchers have found two sixteenth-century anchors in the area but no evidence of a vessel. Recent land excavations at La Navidad, the site of Columbus's ill-fated fort, may help pinpoint this famous shipwreck.

In 1493, on his second expedition to the Americas, Columbus took seventeen ships carrying colonists and supplies. Not far from La Navidad, he established La Isabela, the first European town in America. He sent twelve vessels back to Spain, and later, four of the five remaining ships sank during hurricanes. Since the early 1980s, researchers have used mechanical and electronic tools to survey and map the bay at La Isabela. Their findings suggest that wrecks from Columbus's colony are buried deeply in soft sediments.

Christopher Columbus's fourth voyage in 1502 was the most remarkable. For a year, his four **caravels** cruised the

Recycled Remains

La India, the first European ship constructed in the Americas, was built from the vessels wrecked during hurricanes at La Isabela.

Land archaeologists have studied the remains of Christopher Columbus's house on a cliff overlooking the bay at La Isabela.

19

Vessels That Paved the Way

As the Age of Exploration dawned, Portugal and Spain were perfecting two ship types—the caravel and the nao (above). These were the first European watercraft able to make round-trip voyages in the Atlantic and Indian Oceans. The fast, easily maneuverable caravel was ideal for exploration; the larger, slower nao carried cargo. Shipwrights built these vessels using their experience instead of a set of plans. Eventually, larger craft that could supply and defend colonies replaced caravels and naos. Few documents have been found that explain how vessels of exploration were constructed. Archaeologists are learning about caravels and naos from examples on the seabed.

east coast of Central America, seeking a sea route to the Orient. During an attack by native peoples, he had to abandon one ship at the Belén River in Panama. He left another ship behind because wood-eating marine worms had destroyed its hull. When his two remaining worm-eaten vessels were close to sinking, Columbus ran them onto a beach on the north coast of Jamaica. He and his 115 crewmen lived in huts on the ships until they were rescued a year later.

Searching for Columbus

In the early 1980s, researchers at the Institute of Nautical Archaeology (INA) in Texas began a project to study discovery-era ships. Their work was unique because it focused on Columbus's wrecks and other sixteenth-century vessels of exploration.

In 1982, an INA team began to search St. Ann's Bay, Jamaica, where Columbus was marooned and where his son settled Sevilla la Nueva, or New Seville, a few years later. The

In St. Ann's Bay, Jamaica, researchers from one project tow a magnetometer to search for metallic objects under the sand in the shallow water.

site of New Seville, surrounded by English plantation ruins from the 1700s, was located in 1935. The shoreline had changed so much that land encircled the plantation's stone pier. The crew searched offshore first, using a **magnetometer** and other electronic tools to scan above and below the seabed. They found many wrecks, but none from the 1500s. They suspected that the pier was built on debris from Columbus's caravels. To test this theory, they put metal tubes, 4 feet (1.2 m) wide, next to the pier and dug down inside them, removing rubble and watery sand with a suction device called a **dredge**. They found English artifacts 20 feet (6 m) deep but no trace of Columbus's ships.

The hunt for *La Gallega*, the caravel that Columbus abandoned in Panama, began from an airplane in 1987. Researchers tried to match the view from the sky with descriptions of the Belén River written by people on Columbus's last voyage. On land, the archaeologists used high-tech tools to look for the wreck and a camp that Columbus's men had established. They found pieces of sixteenth-century Spanish pottery not far from shore. They mapped the riverbed and probed below its surface with electronic and mechanical tools. Team members located several targets for future examination. But for now, *La Gallega* remains hidden by the sands of time.

Other Shipwreck Sites

The INA team also studied wrecks at Bahía Mujeres in Mexico, Molasses Reef in the Turks and Caicos Islands, and High-

What Is a Mag?

A mag, short for magnetometer, is an instrument that measures changes in Earth's magnetic field and detects the presence of objects containing iron. Mags are commonly used to search for shipwrecks.

born Cay in the Bahamas. The archaeologists hoped to discover the identities and dates of the sites through fieldwork and archival research. In addition, if pieces of the wooden hulls had survived, they hoped to learn how early ships of exploration had been built.

After the Bahía Mujeres wreck was discovered in 1958, divers and amateur archaeologists brought the cannons and anchors to shore. The site was then forgotten until 1983, when INA joined Mexican marine archaeologists to study the objects recovered from the site. They concluded that these items dated from the early sixteenth century. In 1984, the team

Underwater metal detectors in use at the Bahía Mujeres wreck in 1983

Molasses Reef project team members use air bags to "walk" a heavy iron cannon to the lifting area.

relocated and mapped the wreck's coral-covered ballast in 10 feet (3 m) of water, but they found nothing to reveal the ship's identity. Until more research is carried out underwater and in archives, Mexico's oldest shipwreck will remain a mystery.

Work at Molasses Reef produced more favorable results. In 1976, treasure hunters discovered the wreck in 20 feet (6 m) of water. When INA scientists began their research in 1982, the wreck had been looted and harmed by explosives. Despite the damage, archaeologists recorded and excavated the site thoroughly. Amid 40 tons of ballast, they found 10 tons of artifacts—including pottery, ship's hardware, weapons, and other objects. For nine years, researchers treated and analyzed these items at a conservation lab in Texas. The artifacts and project records now reside at the Turks and Caicos National Museum.

From the artifacts, amount of ballast, and pattern of objects on the seabed, archaeologists determined that the ship was a medium-sized Spanish caravel or nao with three masts, about 60 feet (18 m) long and 20 feet (6 m) wide. It was heavily armed but carried little cargo. Artifacts from the late 1400s and early 1500s suggested that the vessel sank before 1530, making it the oldest known wreck in the Americas. However, archaeologists still don't know the ship's name or purpose.

At the Highborn Cay wreck, a white rope grid was laid over the site for mapping purposes.

Because most of the wooden hull was gone, researchers gathered few clues about how the Molasses Reef ship was built. The Highborn Cay wreck helped sove this question. In 1965, sport divers located the ballast pile, anchors, and cannons in 20 feet (6 m) of water. They decided to **salvage** many items, some of which came to the attention of the INA team. Similarities between the Highborn Cay and Molasses Reef sites prompted the archaeologists to request permission to conduct a survey in 1983 and to excavate in 1986.

The salvors had removed ballast in the bow and **stern**. This exposed parts of the wooden hull, which forces of nature eroded over time. However, as the wreck settled, it left grooves in the seabed that could be mapped even though the wood was gone. In addition to recording the hull remains, team members excavated a trench across the middle of the ballast. Beneath the pile of rocks, they discovered well-preserved parts of the ship that helped them to figure out the construction of sixteenth-century vessels.

Underwater archaeologists have excavated other sixteenth-century wrecks in Texas, Florida, Canada, the Azores Islands, the Caribbean, Portugal, and England. Although most of these ships were used for commerce or colonization, they were similar to vessels of exploration. Archaeologists are examining new sites and historic documents to learn more about how ships of the era were built and outfitted. Nonetheless, each wreck has its own clues and mysteries for archaeologists to solve in their efforts to reassemble the puzzles of the past.

Italian explorer John Cabot in Newfoundland

Chapter Four

A New Land to Explore

Did Columbus ever realize that he had reached the Americas rather than Asia? We can't answer this question, but we do know that his voyages caused many Europeans to sail west to find the East. Because Spain quickly dominated the central and southern parts of the Americas, England and France turned their sights in another direction. Their mariners searched North America for a northwest passage to the Orient, opening the door to settlement and trade in what is now eastern Canada and northeastern United States.

English Enterprise

John Cabot, an Italian explorer hired by the English, reached North America in 1497. He and eighteen crewmen landed in Newfoundland and explored as far south as New England. They were the first Europeans since the Vikings to see this part of the Americas. On his second expedition in 1498, Cabot and his four ships vanished. A decade later, Sebastian Cabot continued his father's quest by exploring the east coasts of North and South America.

Between 1607 and 1610, Henry Hudson tried four times to find a northwest passage. On his first expedition, he sailed

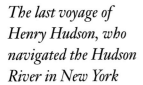

The last voyage of Henry Hudson, who navigated the Hudson River in New York

closer to the North Pole than any previous explorer. Land that he claimed on his third voyage, which was financed by Holland, enabled the Dutch to settle New York. Unfortunately, his fourth trip was his undoing. Hudson's ship became frozen in ice in the bay that now bears his name. After a terrible winter, his crew **mutinied** and cast Hudson and seven loyal sailors adrift in a small boat, never to be heard from again.

French Ventures

France was also eager to find a northwest route to Asia. In 1524, it sponsored Italian mariner Giovanni da Verrazano, who surveyed the Atlantic seaboard between present-day North Carolina and Newfoundland. Jacques Cartier made three voyages to southeastern Canada between 1534 and 1542. In 1603, Samuel de Champlain explored from Canada to New England. In 1608, he sailed down the St. Lawrence River, founded France's first permanent North American colony in Quebec, and scouted the upper Great Lakes.

René-Robert Cavelier, Sieur de La Salle

The most persistent French explorer was René-Robert Cavelier, Sieur de La Salle, who hoped to find a course to the Orient while establishing trade along the inland waterways of North America. He explored the lower Great Lakes and the Illinois River south to the Mississippi River, founding four forts along the way. After canoeing down the Mississippi to the Gulf of Mexico in 1682, he claimed the territory for France and named it Louisiana.

An Ambitious Mission

La Salle then devised a plan to find a sea route to the Mississippi, build forts along the Gulf Coast, and attack Spanish outposts in Mexico. He left France in 1684 with four ships and 300 people. After one vessel was lost to pirates, the fleet missed the mouth of the Mississippi River and landed 500 miles (805 km) west at Matagorda Bay, Texas, in 1685. One ship, *La Belle*, entered the bay safely, but the cargo vessel *L'Aimable* was wrecked. After the third ship was sent back to France, the ill-supplied survivors built a fort.

La Salle left to explore the area. During his absence, *La Belle* sank in a storm in January 1686. When he returned, he tried to save the colony by leading a rescue expedition to a French fort in the north, but his own men killed him along the way. Indians later slayed the remaining settlers.

In 1995, researchers at the Texas Historical Commission found the remains of *La Belle* 12 miles (19 km) offshore in 15 feet (4.6 m) of water. Using historic accounts and reports from local fishermen, team members surveyed the bay with a magnetometer. When divers investigated one of the mag targets, they found a cannon and other artifacts from La Salle's time. A murky and unpredictable bay made excavation difficult,

however. The archaeologists decided to build a watertight enclosure called a **cofferdam** around the wreck, pump out the water inside, and excavate the site as if it were on dry land.

Artifacts excavated in 1996 and 1997 reflected *La Belle*'s dual role to explore and colonize. The cargo included thousands of beads, bells, rings, and straight pins for trade with Native Americans. Weapons, tools, pottery, bottles, utensils, personal effects, and wooden casks used to carry supplies revealed details about the ship and its passengers. Other well-

These cannonballs were excavated from the La Belle *site.*

33

Unique Excavation

The cofferdam around *La Belle* consisted of two concentric steel walls that rested on the seabed and rose 12 feet (3.7 m) above the sea surface. After the water inside was pumped out, archaeologists had a clear view of the abundant, complex wreck remains. The space between the inner and outer walls was filled with sand and rock. This created a deck for project operations and gear, including a crane used to lift objects out of the cofferdam.

preserved items included a leather wallet, shoes, and a human skeleton lying on a huge pile of rope. Archaeologists recorded the remains of the hull very carefully before and after removing them. After conservation and analysis, artifacts and the reconstructed hull will be displayed so that everyone can learn about La Salle's epic adventure.

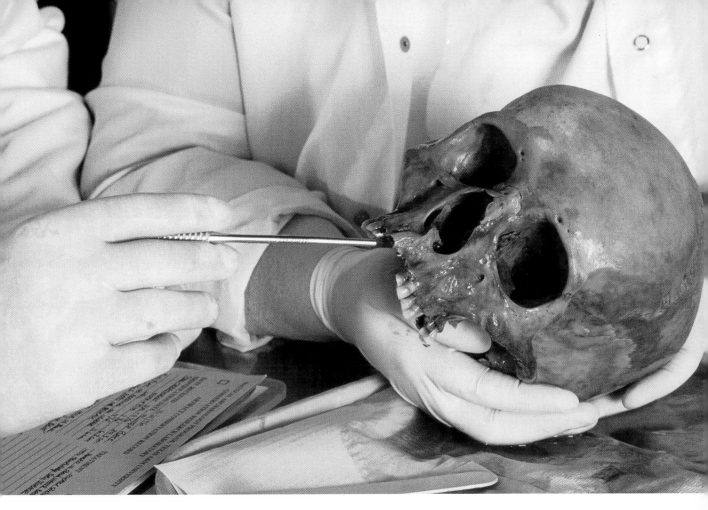

Spanish Sails

Spaniards began to explore the Gulf of Mexico and southeastern North America in 1513. They tried unsuccessfully to establish colonies until 1565, when St. Augustine was founded on the east coast of La Florida. At the same time, the discovery of a sea route from the Philippines to Mexico prompted Spain to investigate the west coast of the continent.

Spanish ships seeking Oriental goods could sail due west from Mexico, but winds and currents kept them from returning by the same route. Mariners finally learned that if they first

Archaeologists examine a human skull recovered from the La Belle *wreck.*

What Is a Galleon?

A galleon is a large, square-rigged sailing ship of the fifteenth to early eighteenth centuries. The Spanish used this type of ship for war and commerce.

sailed north to Japan, they could cross the Pacific Ocean on a straight course. After landing at present-day Oregon or northern California, they headed south for Spanish ports. Once this route was established, Manila **galleon** fleets made the crossing regularly, although the journey was difficult and dangerous. The trip from east to west took about three months, but the voyage home could take three times as long. Weather-beaten and weary crews needed a safe haven on the west coast where they could rest before traveling on to Mexico.

Sebastian Cermeño, commander of the galleon *San Agustín*, was charged with finding a reliable harbor for the returning Pacific fleets. The galleon left the Philippines in 1595 with eighty people and 130 tons of cargo. After reaching northern California, Cermeño began to explore the coast before turning south. But while the *San Agustín* was anchored in Drake's Bay, heavy seas and winds sank it.

Archaeologists were excavating an Indian village at Drake's Bay in the early 1940s when they came across evidence of the wreck. They found iron ship's spikes and pieces of late-sixteenth-century Chinese porcelain. Later excavations produced more pottery, buttons, and iron bolts. Researchers concluded that the native peoples had acquired these items from wreckage and cargo that had washed ashore. Historical research identified the *San Agustín* as the likely source.

Others have searched unsuccessfully for the wreck since 1965. Some believe the ship is buried in as much as 15 feet (4.6 m) of sand. In 1982, underwater archaeologists from the U.S. National Park Service surveyed the bay with a magnetometer and found promising targets. Since 1996, research divers have examined many of these sites and found other wrecks but not the *St. Agustín*. Nonetheless, after heavy winter storms, bits of Chinese porcelain are still found washed up on the beach. They are tantalizing clues that suggest the only known wreck of a galleon in the United States rests nearby.

Jean-François de
Galaup, Comte de
La Pérouse

Chapter Five

An Uncharted Expanse

Jean-François de Galaup, Comte (Count) de La Pérouse, handed a packet of mail, a log of his recent travels, and a letter detailing his future destinations to British First Fleet captain Arthur Phillip. La Pérouse and his men had been gathering scientific data at sea for three years when they encountered the fleet at Botany Bay, Australia, on January 24, 1788. He planned to continue exploring Pacific islands before returning to France in early 1789. Phillip, who was there to

Where in the World Are We?

Determining longitude—how far a ship had sailed east or west—was an obstacle to early mariners. They could calculate latitude—their location north or south of the equator—with navigational tools that measured the positions of the sun or the stars. But they could only estimate the distance that they had sailed. The invention of a shipboard clock called the marine chronometer (above) in 1759 helped seafarers tell how long they had been sailing and therefore how far they had sailed.

establish an English colony, promised to forward the mail to France.

La Pérouse stayed six weeks at Botany Bay while his crew made scientific observations, took on water and firewood, and repaired their ships, the *Boussole* and the *Astrolabe*. They departed on March 10, 1789, and were never heard from again.

New Reasons to Explore

From 1650 to 1750, oceanic exploration dwindled as nations took stock of what they had gained during the past 200 years. Colonies and commerce had been established. Settlers instead of discoverers were going to sea. The design, outfitting, and stocking of ships also had improved. A new era of maritime exploration began, driven by a desire for knowledge instead of expansion. Led mostly by England and France, expeditions became well-planned ventures that included scientists as part of their crews.

Filled with thousands of islands in clusters and in isolation, the Pacific

Ocean presented a new universe for exploration. Although charts of the Pacific existed, the locations of many landforms were incorrect. As Europeans ventured into this watery expanse, many islands were rediscovered, reclaimed, and renamed.

A Fateful Challenge

Inspired by the remarkable voyages of the English captain James Cook between 1768 and 1780, French king Louis XVI ordered La Pérouse to undertake a four-year global circumnavigation. Nothing was left to chance. When the *Boussole* and

In 1785, Louis XVI ordered La Pérouse to circumnavigate the globe for France.

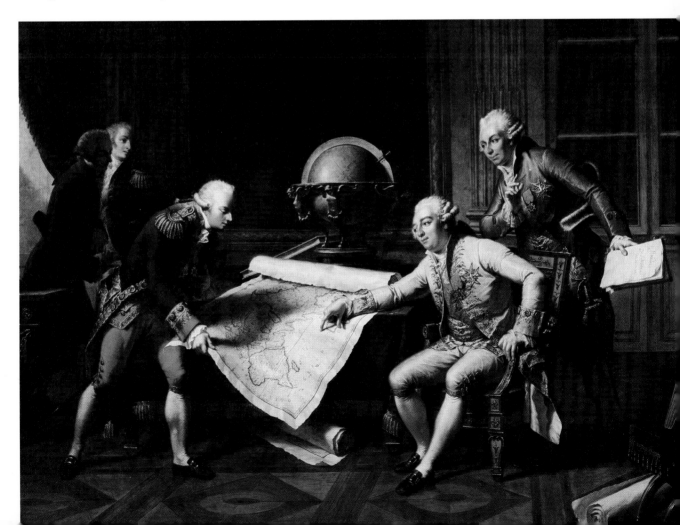

the *Astrolabe* departed, they carried the best maps, equipment, supplies, scientists, and mariners. They went from the Atlantic into the Pacific, to Alaska via Easter Island and Hawaii, down the west coast of North America, across the Pacific to Asia, and up the coast of China to Russia. Here La Pérouse found orders from France to make his fateful trip to Australia.

When La Pérouse hadn't returned to France by late 1789, officials sent search missions, but they found no trace. The mystery didn't begin to unravel until 1827. Based on local stories about two ships wrecked in a storm, castaways, and salvaged artifacts, an English captain visited Vanikoro Island, northeast of Botany Bay. He bartered for French-made items that later were linked to La Pérouse. In the late 1950s, divers found the remains of the ships on a reef at Vanikoro.

Telltale Finds

In 1986, the Queensland Museum in Australia organized a project to examine the two wrecks as well as a camp onshore where survivors had built a boat from salvaged timbers and sailed away, never to be seen again. One wreck, strewn along a slope 35 to 200 feet (11 to 61 m) deep, had cannons, anchors, and iron bars on the surface.

When archaeologists vacuumed away sand and coral with a dredge, they uncovered bronze medallions, trade beads, shoe buckles, coins, broken china, a silver plate, and a brass helmet. The most exciting discoveries were mineral, fossil, and botanical specimens and a cask containing a seashell collection gathered by the expedition's scientists.

The second wreck, located inside a shallow break in the reef, produced pewter plates and mugs, glass beads, cut glass gemstones, brass throat armor called gorgets, and scientific and navigational instruments. Archaeologists found evidence of the camp onshore.

Based on the nature and distribution of wreckage, archaeologists suspect that the first, deeper site is La Pérouse's flagship, the *Boussole*, which crashed violently and left only four survivors. The *Astrolabe* apparently ran aground while trying to help the other ship and more of its crew was able to reach the safety of shore.

Important Reports

La Pérouse left an officer in Russia to travel overland with expedition documents. Those records have provided valuable details about his voyage.

Arctic and Antarctic exploration often ended in failure—or death. No lives were lost, however, after the Endurance became trapped in ice during an expedition led by British explorer Ernest Shackleton.

Chapter Six

The Cold Hinterlands

"25th April 1848. HM Ships Terror and Erebus were deserted on the 22nd April, 5 leagues NNW of this, having been beset [by ice] since 12th Sept. 1846. The officers and crews consisting of 105 souls under the command of Captain F. R. M. Crozier landed. . . . Sir John Franklin died on the 11th June 1847."

Found in 1859, this grim message offered clues to the fate of one of England's most celebrated polar explorers. On a mission to map a northwest passage

45

Long-Sought Success

The first person to traverse the entire Northwest Passage in a single voyage was Norwegian Roald Amundsen. The trip lasted from 1903 to 1906. Amundsen also set a record in 1911, when he became the first person to reach the South Pole.

from the Atlantic to the Pacific, John Franklin, 128 crewmen, and their ships, the HMS *Erebus* and the HMS *Terror*, disappeared in the Arctic Ocean in 1845. Search parties sent to look for Franklin found a trail of frozen bodies, skeletons, and abandoned gear that testified to a tragic end.

Arctic Exploration

From the mid-1500s, explorers traveling by ship tried to pierce the Arctic's icy armor. Initially, they sought trade routes across the top of Asia and the Americas, but in the 1800s, interest focused on scientific research, particularly in North America. Expeditions to map the islands and waterways at the northern limits of the continent embarked regularly. Eventually, the course of the Northwest Passage became evident, although conditions prevented anyone from traveling the passage in a single voyage. Research was often conducted from vessels drifting in ice, and numerous ships were abandoned after they were damaged or crushed by ice.

Grim Remains

Search parties began to look for Franklin in 1848, but no evidence emerged until 1850, when artifacts, graves, and building remains were found at the expedition's first camp. Four years later, an Arctic surveyor learned from Inuit hunters that starving white men had been seen walking south after abandoning their ice-locked ships. The Inuit produced English artifacts and suggested that the men had resorted to cannibalism—the practice of eating human flesh. Other searches found additional corpses and a bizarre array of items that the men had lugged across the frozen wasteland.

Recent studies of the human remains have revealed some interesting facts. Bones cut with a metal knife support the claim that the desperate men resorted to cannibalism. Remaining

Human bones with knife marks found by Canadian archaeologists suggest that John Franklin's crew may have practiced cannibalism.

A National Resource

Because they hold clues to the Franklin expedition, the *Terror* and the *Erebus* have been declared wrecks of national historic importance in Canada.

bones and tissues contained high levels of lead. The expeditions had carried food in tins sealed with lead, which contaminated the contents. As the men ate, they were slowly poisoned, which affected their physical and mental health.

In 1997, Parks Canada archaeologists used electronic tools to search for the *Terror* and the *Erebus*. While they found no evidence of the ships underwater, they did find related artifacts on land at camps that Inuit seal hunters have used for centuries. A project is underway to record Inuit folklore about the expedition since these legends may help locate the site of the ships and provide further details about the disaster.

Arctic Archaeology

Although numerous ships were lost during polar exploration, little underwater archaeology has been conducted because of the difficult conditions. Canadian and U.S. archaeologists undertook the first detailed study of an Arctic wreck in 1995–1996 near Victoria Island. Intact and mostly submerged, the *Baymaud* wreck is a unique example of a small group of wooden ships built to withstand the stresses of a polar environment.

The ship was built as the *Maud* in 1917 for explorer Roald Amundsen. He planned to drift across the North Pole to prove that a vessel could freeze into the ice and serve as a floating research station. Although he didn't achieve these goals during his 1918–1925 expedition, Amundsen did complete the second successful crossing of the Northeast Passage along the

top of Russia. Because of the gathered scientific data, the mission was one of the most important research projects ever conducted in the Arctic. In 1925, the *Maud* was sold, renamed the *Baymaud*, and used as a supply ship, floating warehouse, and wireless station until it sank at its moorings in 1930.

The Maud, *led by Roald Amundsen, returned from its travels in the Arctic in 1925.*

The Southern Extreme

Mariners began to explore the southern end of the earth in the 1700s. By the early 1900s, men had camped on the Antarctic continent. They were also mapping the coastlines, studying the frozen interior, and competing to reach the South Pole.

Ships could penetrate the ice-clogged waters around Antarctica during only a few months a year. As in the Arctic, vessels were in peril of being trapped in the ice. This is what happened to the *Endurance*.

Sir Ernest Shackleton and his twenty-seven crew members planned to cross the continent on foot, but in February 1915 their vessel became icebound, just a day from its landing site. The men lived on board as the ice pack drifted and slowly crushed the hull. In October, they abandoned the *Endurance*, which sank a month later. At first, they lived on the ice near the ship, but later they sailed their salvaged lifeboats and provisions to a more secure location. Shackleton and a small crew then sailed a lifeboat 800 miles (1,287 km) to find help. When they returned in August, every crew member had survived. No attempts have been made to find the remains of the *Endurance*.

Opposite: Underwater archaeologists continue to learn from shipwrecks of the explorers.

Chapter Seven

A New Challenge

Only a fraction of the ships lost in the last 500 years of global exploration have been studied by underwater archaeologists. This is partly due to the newness of the discipline and the relatively small number of trained professionals. In addition, many exploration vessels were lost in harsh circumstances and frontier environments, and their remains have been altered or destroyed. And when only a few pieces have survived, it can be impossible to tell a ship's function. Vessels of discovery represent a new area of study, and archaeologists are still developing research strategies and models. Every wreck they study helps them to reconstruct a timeline of water travel.

Technology has played an important role in the search for maritime history. Archaeologists can now find sites that are buried under the seabed and study sites that are thousands of feet deep. New tools allow them to recover more information from wrecks.

Who knows what will be possible in the future? One thing is certain: there are many vessels in the waters of the world waiting to be explored. Young people can get involved by learning about ships, maritime cultures, and efforts to map the globe. Today, you can be a shipwreck steward who treats sites responsibly, and in the future, you can be an underwater archaeologist who reveals their mysteries. Along the way, you also will learn what it means to explore.

Glossary

archaeologists—scientists who study past cultures based on artifacts and other evidence left behind

archives—collections of public documents and the buildings in which they are kept

artifacts—objects made or modified by humans

ballast—heavy material such as rocks or pieces of iron placed in the lower part of a ship for stability

bow—the front or forward end of a ship

caravels—small, maneuverable ships used for exploration in the fifteenth and sixteenth centuries

circumnavigated—traveled completely around

cofferdam—an enclosure that can be placed around a shipwreck to make an excavation easier to conduct

conservation—the documentation, analysis, cleaning, and treatment of an object to ensure its survival

cultures—groups of people with distinctive institutions, tools, customs, rituals, and beliefs

dredge—a suction device used to remove mud and sand underwater

excavate—to scientifically recover and study the remains of past human activity

features—evidence of human activity at an archaeological site

galleon—a large, square-rigged sailing ship

hull—the body of a ship

magnetometer—an electronic instrument that measures changes in Earth's magnetic field

mutinied—refused to obey authority; rebelled

nao (pronounced NOW)—a cargo vessel used in many early voyages of exploration

salvage—to recover items from a shipwreck without using scientific instruments

shipwrights—people who build or repair boats

stern—the back or rear end of a ship

To Find Out More

Books

Armstrong, Jennifer. *Shipwreck at the Bottom of the World: Shackleton's Amazing Voyage*. New York: Crown, 1998.

Coulter, Tony. *Jacques Cartier, Samuel de Champlain, and the Explorers of Canada*. New York: Chelsea House, 1993.

Gleiter, Jan. *Christopher Columbus*. Austin, Tex.: Raintree/Steck-Vaughn, 1996.

Johnstone, Michael. *The History News: Explorers*. Cambridge, Mass.: Candlewick Press, 1997.

Lerner Geography Department. *Sunk!: Exploring Underwater Archaeology*. Minneapolis: Runestone Press, 1994.

Tritton, Roger, ed. *The Visual Dictionary of Ships and Sailing*. New York: Dorling Kindersley, 1991.

Organizations and Online Sites

Archaeological Institute of America
656 Beacon Street
Boston, MA 02215–2010
http://www.archaeological.org/
This website offers up-to-date information about the archaeology profession.

British Sub-Aqua Club
Telford's Quay
Ellesmere Port, South Wirral
Cheshire L65 4FY, England
http://www.bsac.com/
This website provides information about learning to dive.

Explorers of the Millennium Website
1900 Stratford Road
Highland Park, IL 60035
http://tqjunior.advanced.org/4034
This website, created by students at Sherwood Elementary School, features a timeline and a quiz.

Institute of Nautical Archaeology
P.O. Drawer HG
College Station, TX 77841–5137
http://nautarch.tamu.edu/ina/
This website provides information about the institute's projects.

The Mariners' Museum
100 Museum Drive
Newport News, VA 23606
http://www.mariner.org/age/index.html
This website offers information about the Age of Exploration, including images, video, and useful links.

Ships of Discovery
Corpus Christi Museum of Science and History
1900 N. Chaparral
Corpus Christi, TX 78401
http://shipsofdiscovery.org/
This website offers information about Columbus's lost ships, artifact conservation, and experimental archaeology.

A Note on Sources

For years, I've been interested in the voyages of explorers to various parts of the globe. Consequently, I have collected many books, articles, and newspaper clippings on this subject. Over the years, my husband and I have acquired many books related to underwater archaeology. When I began to write *Shipwrecks of the Explorers*, I reviewed many of these materials to refresh my memory. I also relied on experiences that I acquired as a member of some of the projects that I have written about in this book.

But my personal resources couldn't provide all of the information that I needed. I telephoned archaeologists who had worked on the projects to seek their firsthand knowledge and advice. I also searched on the Internet when I needed up-to-date details or quick facts about certain shipwrecks.

And, of course, I pored over books, especially ones about global exploration. They helped me to understand specific events as well as the larger picture of discovery worldwide.

My experience writing this book offers a good tip for kids. If you are interested in a topic, become involved in related activities and collect as many books as you can about the subject. Practical knowledge and a personal library are resources that you will rely on again and again.

—*KC Smith*

Index

Numbers in *italics* indicate illustrations.

About the Author

Since 1976, KC Smith has worked on underwater archaeological projects in the United States, the Caribbean, and Africa. As program supervisor at the Museum of Florida History in Tallahassee, she develops educational programs about history, archaeology, and folklife. KC Smith is a charter member of the Society for American Archaeology Public Education Committee and coedits its publication, *Teaching with Archaeology*. She has also edited the Institute of Nautical Archaeology newsletter.

KC Smith has studied humanities, archaeology, and history at Florida Atlantic University, Texas A & M University, and Florida State University. Her interest in shipwrecks comes from helping her husband Roger, an underwater archaeologist, with research projects. She believes that the findings from such projects should be shared with the public, especially young people. KC Smith is the author of the Watts Library books *Exploring for Shipwrecks* and *Ancient Shipwrecks*.